S0-BYZ-236

TO TEACHER-

- -

FROM-

- -

DATE:

❀

- -

Blessings for a #1 Teacher

© 2012 Christian Art Gifts, RSA
      Christian Art Gifts Inc., IL, USA

First edition 2012
Second edition 2016

Designed by Christian Art Gifts

Images used under license from Shutterstock.com

Scripture quotations are taken from the Holy Bible, New International Version® NIV®. Copyright © 1973, 1978, 1984, 2011 by Biblica, Inc.® Used by permission. All rights reserved worldwide.

Scripture quotations are taken from the New King James Version. Copyright © 1979, 1980, 1982 by Thomas Nelson, Inc. Used by permission. All rights reserved.

Scripture quotations are taken from the Contemporary English Version. Copyright © 1995 by American Bible Society. All rights reserved.

Scripture quotations are taken from THE MESSAGE. Copyright © by Eugene H. Peterson, 1993, 1994, 1995, 1996, 2000, 2001, 2002 by NavPress Publishing Group. Used by permission.

Printed in China

ISBN 978-1-4321-1339-1

Christian Art Gifts has made every effort to trace the ownership of all quotes and poems in this book. In the event of any question that may arise from the use of any quote or poem, we regret any error made and will be pleased to make the necessary correction in future editions of this book.

© All rights reserved. No part of this book may be reproduced in any form without permission in writing from the publisher, except in the case of brief quotations in critical articles or reviews.

16   17   18   19   20   21   22   23   24   25   –   10   9   8   7   6   5   4   3   2   1

BLESSINGS

FOR A
#1 TEACHER

† christian
art gifts®

A TEACHER'S PRAYER

LORD, PLEASE HELP ME
TO STRENGTHEN THEIR VOICES,
BODIES & MINDS,
TO EXPRESS THEIR FEELINGS
AND CONTROL THEM SOMETIMES.
TO EXPLORE WHAT'S NEAR
AND VENTURE AFAR,
BUT MOST IMPORTANT
to love who they are.

You're a *special* person!
A teacher who truly *cares*.
Know that you're *appreciated*,
and *daily* in my prayers.

– Karla Dornacher –

He shall *give* His angels
charge over you, to keep
you in all your *ways*.

– Psalm 91:11 –

Be of good *courage*, and He
shall *strengthen* your heart,
all you who *hope* in the LORD.

– Psalm 31:24 –

February 2017

S	M	T	W	T	F	S
			1	2	3	4
5	6	7	8	9	10	11
12	13	14	15	16	17	18
19	20	21	22	23	24	25
26	27	28				

Sat | **Sun**
18 | **19**

the BIG BANG THEORY™

THE BIG BANG THEORY and all related characters and elements ⊚ & ™ Warner Bros. Entertainment Inc. (s16)

An **APPLE**
lasts a short time
in the hand of a teacher.
A bit of **WISDOM** lasts
a lifetime in the mind
of a child.

Your LOVE has given
me GREAT JOY and
ENCOURAGEMENT.

– Philemon 7 –

Time spent with children
is NEVER wasted.

School is a building that has four walls – with tomorrow inside.

– Lon Watters –

Love is a better teacher than duty.

– Albert Einstein –

Wisdom is more precious than rubies.

– Proverbs 8:11 –

Love is a great teacher.

– St. Augustine –

In matters of style, swim with the current. In matters of principle, stand like a rock.

– Thomas Jefferson –

You make a difference!

Every child is
a bundle of potential
and promise.

Commit to the LORD
whatever you do, and
He will establish your plans.

– Proverbs 16:3 –

Do all the good you can,
by all the means you can,
in all the ways you can,
in all the places you can,
to all the people you can,
as long as ever you can.

- John Wesley -

All our children deserve teachers
who believe they can learn and who will
not be satisfied until they do.

- Joe Nathan -

YOU ARE
God's
handiwork,

CREATED

in Christ Jesus
TO DO GOOD WORKS,
which God
prepared in advance
FOR YOU to do.

Ephesians 2:10

Kites rise

HIGHEST

against the wind,
not with it.

- Winston Churchill -

Teachers believe they have a
GIFT FOR GIVING:
it drives them with the same
irrepressible drive that drives
others to create a work of art
or a market or a building.

- A. Bartlett Giamatti -

GOOD

Train up a child in the way
he should go, and when he is old
he will not depart from it.

- Proverbs 22:6 -

"I will instruct you and teach
you in the way you should go;
I will counsel you with
My loving eye on you."

- Psalm 32:8 -

To **TEACH**,
to guide, to explain,
to help, to nurture –
these are life's
noblest attainments.

– Frank Tyger –

Seven days without prayer makes one weak.

- Allen E. Bartlett -

He who opens a school door, closes a prison.

- Victor Hugo -

AN APPLE A DAY

A Recipe for an Excellent Teacher:

A is for aptitude –
    intelligence to teach

P is for patience –
    when they're hard to reach

P is for prayer –
    when my day's work is done

L is for love –
    may I love everyone

E is for empathy –
    a feeling heart.

Mix them together –
    and now we can start.

– Melody Carlson –

Children are
MESSENGERS we
send to a time
we will not see.

I have not stopped
GIVING THANKS for you,
remembering
you in my prayers.

- Ephesians 1:16 -

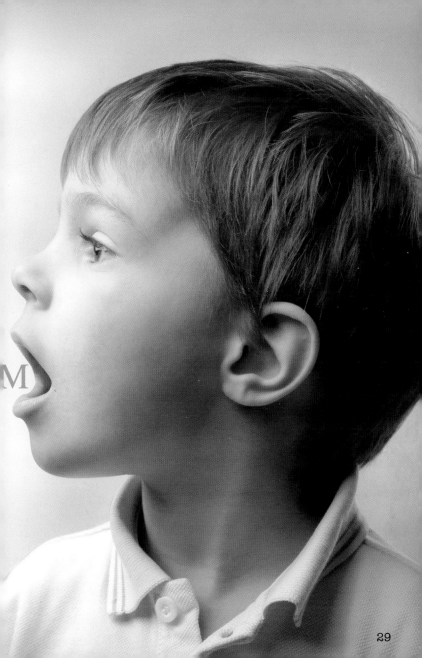

M

*

2

9

5

3

{ Teaching kids to
count is fine,
but teaching them
what counts is best.

- Bob Talbert -

4

2

7

3

SHINE

as lights among
the people of this world,
as you hold firmly to the
message that gives life.

- Philippians 2:15-16 -

To teach is
to learn twice.

- Joseph Joubert -

A TEACHER affects eternity;
he can never tell where
his influence stops.

- Henry Adams -

Whatever your hand

finds to do, do it

with all your might.

- Ecclesiastes 9:10 -

A good teacher remembers
what it was like to be taught
by their favorite teacher.

– Robert McLain –

Whatever you do,
work at it with
ALL YOUR HEART,
as working for the Lord,
not for human masters.

– Colossians 3:23 –

WISDOM

WILL ENTER YOUR

HEART

AND KNOWLEDGE WILL
BE PLEASANT TO YOUR SOUL.

- Proverbs 2:10 -

Blessed is the hand that prepares a pleasure for a child, for there is no saying when and where it may bloom forth.

– Douglas William Jerrold –

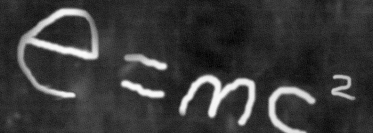

Do not be conformed
to this world,
but be **transformed** by the
renewing of your mind,
that you may prove
what is that good and acceptable
and perfect will of God.

- Romans 12:2 -

God regards with how much
love a person performs
a work, rather than
how much he does.

- Thomas à Kempis -

Be faithful in
small things because it
is in them that your
strength lies.

- Mother Teresa -

In my lifetime I
hope to develop ...
arms that are strong,
hands that are gentle,
ears that will listen,
eyes that are kind,
a mind full of wisdom,
a heart that understands,
a tongue that will
speak softly.

The art of
TEACHING

is the art of

DISCOVERY.

- Mark van Doren -

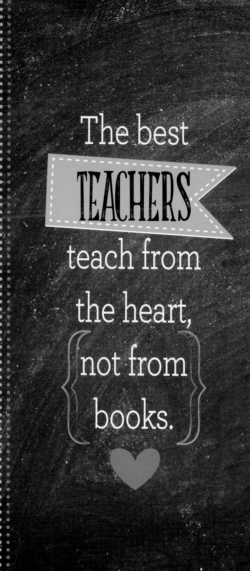

If I can put one touch
of *rosy sunset*
into the life of
any man or woman,
I shall feel that
I have worked with God.

- John MacDonald -

Every time I *think of you*,
I *thank God* for your life.

- 1 Corinthians 1:4 -

People don't care how
much *you know* until they
know how much *you care*.

Kind words can be
short and easy to speak,
but *their echoes*
are truly *endless*.

- Mother Teresa -

GREAT WORKS

are performed
 not by ✓

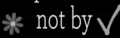
STRENGTH,

but by
PERSEVERANCE.

Samuel Johnson